BIG DESIGNS
FOR SMALL KITCHENS

BIG DESIGNS
FOR SMALL KITCHENS

Marta Serrats

HDi

HARPER DESIGN international

An Imprint of HarperCollinsPublishers

Editorial Director
Nacho Asensio

Texts
Marta Serrats

Translation
Michael Brunelle and Beatriz Cortabarria

Graphic Design & Layout
David Maynar and Mar Nieto

First published in 2004 by:
Harper Design International,
an imprint of HarperCollinsPublishers
10 East 53rd Street
New York, NY 10022

Distributed throughout the world by:
HarperCollins International
10 East 53rd Street
New York, NY 10022
Tel: (212) 207-7000
Fax: (212) 207-7654

HarperCollins books may be purchased for educational, business, or sales promotional use.
For information, please write:
Special Markets Department
HarperCollins Publishers Inc.
10 East 53rd Street
New York, NY 10022

Library of Congress Cataloging-in-Publication Data

Big designs for small kitchens / edited by Marta Serrats.
    p. cm.
Includes index.
ISBN 0-06-073593-7 (hardcover)
1. Kitchens. 2. Small rooms--Decoration. 3. Interior decoration. I. Serrats, Marta.
NK2117.K5B54 2005
747.7'97--dc22
                              2004004325

Editorial Project
Bookslab, S. L.
editorial@bookslab.net
Printed by Gràfiques Ibèria S.A., Barcelona, Spain
D.L.: B-35802-04
First Printing, 2004

Contents

Introduction

Appliances, ranges, oven, counter, extractor hood, cabinet, drawers, waste receptacles, various utensils. . .There are many, many elements of use to us in the kitchen, and an outstanding design and excellent spatial distribution can go a long way toward improving our tasks and exploiting the space we have available for food storage. *Big Designs for Small Kitchens* explores the possibilities open to compact kitchens, which can use their small dimensions to bring together everything necessary for practical, functional use. The three chapters in this volume—New Urban Kitchens, Compact Architecture, and Mobile Compact—analyze, from many different perspectives, the best ideas and applications of compact design.

The kitchen is the room of the house that best defines the trends of a time period. Traditionally, the kitchen played a bit part, kept in the wings as one of the least frequently remembered parts of the house. Today, the high cost of housing has generated a new definition of the idea of habitable space. Rooms blend into a summarily functional whole and are, at the same time, aesthetically pleasing thanks to the precise use of materials that distinctly favor comfort. This tendency to economize on space has led experts to design compact rooms which, like the kitchen, tread on what was once forbidden ground, newly blending dining space with living space.

So what do we want? Perhaps—and here let us leave aside the banal designs of the last few decades, which were sustained by no more than the stylistic pretensions of an elitist generation—we have realized that previous interiors were uncomfortable with themselves. In this sense, it seems that the different disciplines applied to contemporary design are seeking a proper response to that state of affairs, regenerating what was there for a society of high standing.

The term *compact* does not, in these designs, have vanguardist connotations. Compact is the end result of the analysis of a society discontent with itself that now reclaims the ideal of a kitchen made to order, with modules combinable among themselves, a model that guarantees in a minimal space such tasks as food conservation, preparation, and cooking. The refrigerator, the sink, the counter, the work island, all of these elements call for the right distribution.

Today, the kitchen's importance is not measured in feet. It is measured by mixing a series of socio-cultural factors that sum up to the following contemporary response: designs that set out to create a hybrid of functionalism and versatility of materials. It is a formula devised to overcome the disadvantages of concise spaces. And this can only be done if we listen to the needs of our interior spaces. *Big Designs for Small Kitchens* provides plenty of examples that prove that it is possible to have a functional kitchen in a small space.

New Urban Kitchens

New social and technological trends are coming into our homes, giving us a preview of the house of the future. For many, this view represents the abandonment of the traditional concept of home, an abrupt departure from and a destruction of the mold of routine design. The kitchen, of all the spaces in the home, is perhaps the one that has always been most influenced by cultural, social, historic, and even ecological variables. The most recent example of this is the new cosmopolitanism that is being introduced little by little into the dwelling of the new millennium. This cosmopolitanism is embodied in a dynamic society that lives every second to the fullest, for whom time is money and only objects that are functional and satisfy their needs are of use. In response to these modern demands, the new urban kitchens are a reflection of the latest applications in compact, extremely functional designs and super-specialized equipment.

Functionality and the specialization of functions favor the application of new technologies in the kitchen. Even though the idea of operating home appliances with interactive systems controlled by computers can still seem an impossible notion for a large sector of the population, today's advanced designs are already ushering in this lifestyle. Some kitchens integrate microprocessors that will analyze the contents of the refrigerator, program a personalized diet, and even place an order with the supermarket over the Internet, so that groceries are ready upon arriving home after a day at work. This experimentation results in the increased integration of spaces and functional, innovative solutions that take us closer to a singular dwelling. Add to this the evolution of the concept of livability, which, as will be seen in the examples of the next chapter, has encouraged the creation of open spaces in which rooms merge with one another, increasing the capacity for comfort and organization. In these environments, the kitchen disappears and the phenomena of the "e-home," the "intelligent house," emerges.

The tendency to unify environments, however, does not go hand in hand with an increase in livable space; on the contrary, as a consequence of the substantial rise in the cost per square foot in recent years, dwellings tend to be smaller and smaller in a quest for maximum functionality. Kitchens, as independent spaces, are integrated into designs capable of housing the cooking area, with enough room for storing utensils, and even with technological systems that convert the houses of the future into computerized dwellings. Intelligent, compact, and functional kitchens will be converted into highly efficient nerve centers by adapting themselves to the physical conditions of the new urban dwelling of the future.

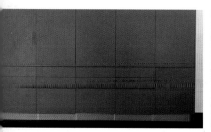

Küche Büro 16

Kurt Lichtblau/Konrad Spindler Architekten
architect
Pez Hejduk
photographer

Innovation and economy of space impress themselves on the character of this module designed by Lichtblau/Spindler Architekten. Conceived as one more furniture component, it stands out by way of its simple, discreet lines, going almost unnoticed as an independent unit when left closed. However, the transformation converts it into a full-fledged range. Its extraordinary effect increases with the system of moveable drawers which, taking advantage of the cubic design of the module, make it easy to keep utensils in order.

A system of multiple moving doors allows the kitchen to be left open when required. As seen in the photograph, the kitchen can be kept closed, leaving open only the space for using the sink.

From left to right, the first cabinet houses the refrigerator, in the center is the ceramic glass cooktop, and at the far right we find the sink. By leaving everything open, we can see the entire kitchen. A small wine storage area can be found on one of the top shelves.

The main elements of a kitchen, like the sink, the cooktop, the coffeemaker, and various shelves for utensils can be found under the upper cabinets. The alternating drawers in the different levels of the module are located in the lower section.

Body Box

Designkoop
architect
Santi Caleca
photographer

Body Box is the foremost example of a "detached" piece of technological furniture that brings together body and clothing care in a single, discreet unit. It integrates essential functions in the clothing care cycle: collecting, sorting, washing, conditioning, tumbling, and even steam/dry cleaning for gentle overnight cleansing of clothes. Input is given via a screen or by remote control, a preview of how all our home electronics will soon be networked.

The second function contained in this unit is body care. A sink with an adjacent shower and steam-bath cabin form the core of this area. Both care modules feature chromotherapy lighting and provide a continuous, gentle curtain of warm air.

A series of Body Box modules providing supplementary or ancillary functions—kitchen, refrigerator-freezer, spa-sauna, and entertainment center—is also conceivable.

BodyBox combines different functions in a single unit: bath, laundry, and kitchen. Above is seen the bath area, which incorporates functions like the sink and a steam bath. The bath is one of the most prevalent spaces in compact design.

All the services are computerized, and the various tasks can be programmed on a central system. The washing machine combines the principal functions of washing, conditioning, and drying.

2 x 60 Kitchen-Studio compacts in Torino

Michele Bonino
architect
Beppe Giardino
photographer

The owner of this house, located only a few minutes from Torino, possesses a passion for gastronomy. This led the architect to design a space that would permit cooking and working in the same space.

A compact piece of furniture was created to serve both functions. The perfectly equipped kitchen is only 23.6 inches (60 centimeters) from the wall; thus the design is resolved by a 3/4-inch by 23.6-inch (2-centimeter by 60-centimeter) module. To write or work, one can sit down comfortably and take advantage of the natural light flowing in from the exterior window. The surface of the desk becomes a bookshelf that can be consulted from this position. In the lower part of the module, a concealed bench was designed for relaxing in the kitchen zone while exquisite culinary delights are being prepared.

An oven, a cooktop, and several cabinets arranged above and below to make efficient use of space are all located on one side of the kitchen. The 2 by 60 module, however, does not have its own plumbing system, and an independent sink was required.

Under the 2 x 60 module, the kitchen includes all the necessary equipment: cooktop, range hood, oven, cabinets for storing products and utensils, and a small stool.

The upper part of the kitchen has been converted into a studio that not only has a desk but also integrates a system of shelves for holding books.

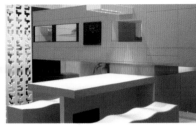

Whirpool / Corian Kitchen of the Future

JAM Design
architect
Rob Carter
photographer

This installation is a responsive living system for a domestic environment. It is a flexible, fully integrated, intelligent, networked product which reacts to a number of emotional and practical everyday requirements. The design highlights aspects such as refrigeration, storage, cleaning, and cooking in a novel way. The result, an "integrated living unit," folds out from a compact rectangle to act as the source of light, sound, and temperature control—a communications terminal as well as a place to come together.

The commitment of Corian and Whirlpool to this design project, conceived and developed by JAM, Softroom and Linbeck Rausch, demonstrates their technological and material strengths and their vision as leaders in their fields, supporting and envisioning change as well as being an integral part of it. An aluminum sliding door separates the kitchen from the dining room. This solution creates a totally adaptable space that can be left open to encourage communication between both areas. On the other hand, if more intimacy is required, the door becomes a divider between two completely independent spaces. The setting looks very streamlined among a myriad of service areas connected to a central system where tasks are programmed. A cursory look at the unit reveals that functions are distributed along a horizontal axis. On one side, the washing machine and the dryer are placed along a line. The services that are essential to the kitchen, like the oven, microwave, and dining table, are on the opposite axis.

This entire unit is self-sufficient, with a computer-controlled system that centralizes necessary tasks. The washing machine, the light, the temperature, and the sound system can all be controlled from the same place.

   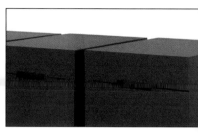

Zoe Kitchen

Disaster Design
architect
Disaster Design
photographer

This kitchen design represents a new concept in domestic space and comfortable living. Its reduced capacity makes it a visibly functional and surprising space. Three apparently independent modules in the form of a box house the compact range. At first sight, its surprising design is closer to a svelte, modern piece of furniture than to that of a traditional range. The three sealed boxes open up via a system of overhead doors that convert into the front of the device, while below, moveable drawers house the cooking utensils. The end result of this novel approach is a compact but fully functional kitchen: in the left-hand box, the faucet; in the central box, the cooking system; in the right-hand box, extra storage space.

The essence of this three-unit compact kitchen system is that the units can be used individually or together. It was designed to use the minimum amount of space while providing basic kitchen services in very small houses that cannot devote a specific area to food preparation.

Geltner Parker Loft

Lewis.Tsurumaki.Lewis
architect
Lewis.Tsurumaki.Lewis
photographer

The architectural team Lewis.Tsurumaki.Lewis was commissioned to refurbish a loft distributed on two levels. This project presented some inconveniences, however, due to the reduced space. The stairs became the primary feature of the renovation, with the kitchen conceived as a stage set for the loft. Dimmable fluorescent tubes in the ceiling provide the necessary lighting for a space set back from the window wall, while a series of stainless-steel counters provide continuity around the kitchen space.

The horizontal extension of the handrail that demarcates the limits of the kitchen makes it possible for a concealed table to extend behind the stair.

The extended railing of the stairway, seen here, was used to create an additional counter in front of the kitchen.

Wohnung Wedekind

Holger Kleine
architect
Werner Huthmacher
photographer

Simple lines counterposed to sinuous curves, pastel tones next to bright colors, and the use of the column as a dividing wall are some of the differentiating elements in this project by Holger Kleine. The architect thus combines the practical side of every kitchen with the originality of the most avant-garde designs to bring about a diaphanous, balanced space.

The balance in this space is created by two completely independent and compact areas. On one side, a unit concealed behind the column can be used for food preparation. The opposite unit is more functional and self-sufficient because it houses a cooking area and has several drawers and cabinets to make tasks easier.

Above is an example of how different heights and combinations of texture were used to impart a dynamic feeling to a small space.

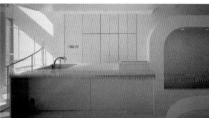

Tango

Norisada Maeda Atelier
architect
Nacása & Partners Inc.
photographer

This project, by Japanese architect Norisada Maeda, is an advanced conception on the combination of public and private spaces. Located at one end of the space, the range grabs our eye because of its pure, neutral, white tone. The workstation and range, contained in a single module of simple lines, blend beautifully with the rest of the suite. Flanking the module, the white wall conceals fitted cabinets, where all the necessary elements can be stored. Finally, the lounge overlaps its circular area in the middle of the room, as is characteristic in Japanese culture.

The white color used throughout the setting is a complete departure from the traditional concept of a kitchen. The color and design of the compact module, as well as the cabinets themselves, are more in tune with a minimalist approach associated with a relaxed setting, like the living room. This perception further enhances the feeling of invisibility consciously created by the architect. The lines between the spaces become neutralized, and the kitchen appears to blend with the surroundings.

Loft Rio Project

Peanutz Architekten
architect
Thomas Bruns
photographer

Urban functional is the term that best defines this loft kitchen, strategically arranged on one side of the space. Open to its setting, it takes advantage of the space between the staircase and the habitable box where the bedroom is located. The quadrangular plan determines the distribution of the U-shaped kitchen, which makes use of the front bar counter to serve the office. The design is notable for its outstanding use of the prolonged stairway, which ends its trajectory with the oven, inside the space.

The main kitchen furnishings include several complementary compartments that help save space, like a small refrigerator for bottles and small containers. The most essential kitchen utensils hang on a steel bar along the front wall. The kitchen's many features are all designed to fulfill their tasks while maintaining a very functional and modern look.

The kitchen uses the square space below the living area. As shown above, the counter, which is used for eating, separates the kitchen area from the rest of the loft.

Inside the small area, the kitchen contains all of the necessary comforts: refrigerator, oven, sink, cooktop, several cupboards combined on various levels, and even a microwave set into the top step of the stairway.

Glasé Kitchen

Moneo Brock Studio
architect
Luis Asín
photographer

The Glasé Kitchen is based on the use of large, sturdy modules. This makes it possible to maximally exploit the storage space and provide easier access to utensils. The varied modulation enables innumerable combinations for unique, tailor-made kitchen arrangements. The work island with Corian sink and counter is center stage, designed to look as if it has eroded with water flow. Two covers partially or fully conceal it, converting the whole island into a flat surface. Mirrored, glossy glass surfaces combine with luminous walls in bright colors. A versatile, functional program dictates simple, continuous lines.

The molded, half-inch Corian countertop has three basins and a drain board. It also has one or two extra Corian lids, which cover the basins and turn the island into a table for preparing food. The piece below with the drawer is made of aluminum. The dimensions of each space can be changed according to need.

The modules can be combined with each other to create a versatile design adapted to the characteristics of each space.

Each module offers numerous combinations with movable shelves and drawers for storing the utensils. The design of the Corian surface stands out in the center.

Tribeca Loft

Moneo Brock Studio
architect
Jordi Miralles
photographer

This loft is on the top floor of a building in New York's Tribeca district. The space is framed in beam-and-column architecture, in a 1,400-square-foot space. The kitchen is under one of the upper crosspieces, a compact, closed, strictly delimited space. The rest of the loft is open, with a skylight overhead. The kitchen uses colorful, textured materials that create a warm setting. Notably, the drawers and shelves mix well and offer the maximum function in the minimal environment granted. The care taken thus multiplies the dual effects of diversity and order.

From inside the module, one has the feeling of being sheltered from the surroundings while being part of them. This is one of the main objectives of this kitchen's compact design. The countertop, containing the cooktop and the fixtures, becomes part of the backdrop. However, each one of the details in this setting forms an integral part of the loft.

A portable module that acts as a worktable defines the limits of the kitchen area. Meanwhile, the group of small cabinets in the kitchen simulates the apparent chaos of the books in the side bookshelf.

Holman House

Dive Architects
architect
Jefferson Smith
photographer

This is a typical 1960s terraced house in a leafy square in south London. The ground floor was divided into rooms, with a former garage-storeroom, a kitchen in the back, and an adjacent, small dining area in a previously existing extension. The idea was to enhance the relationship between the front and the rear, making a large space on the ground floor and incorporating the dining and kitchen areas, as well as a play area. White Formica is used on the long kitchen counter, with a glazed splashback giving the space an aquarium-like feel.

Next to the main door, a cabinet that rises to the ceiling provides the kitchen's largest space for storing food and utensils. The side shelves are arranged at different heights, while the oven, microwave, and larger cabinets for storing necessities are located on the other side.

All the major appliances in this kitchen, like the refrigerator, oven, microwave, and various cabinets and shelves that discreetly keep things in order, compactly fit into the side cube.

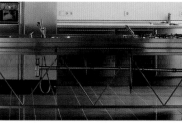

Loftausbau

Heinz Hellermann
architect
Werner Huthmacher
photographer

The remodeling of this large loft enabled the application of an industrial vision of vanguardist design. This compact, conventional system is conceived as a high-tech solution to the needs of the kitchen. In this well-equipped setting, the design links all the necessary elements needed to work in a small space. The use of stainless steel and aluminum is outstanding. Like the rest of the loft, the kitchen is left fully open. The extractor hood reinforces the industrial effect of the whole, as does the extension of the pipes over the ceiling surface. Discreet, cold, and functional, it is a good model for the 21st century.

The main module is a departure from the traditional food preparation system. The cooktop and the fixtures are the product of a conscious industrial approach, resulting in a style that is unique and modern. Even the plumbing system is exposed under the counter, further emphasizing the industrial look of the entire setting.

Loft Beverly Hills

Peanutz Architekten
architect
Thomas Bruns
photographer

This kitchen in the center of the house is perceived as an island in space. Its daring design stands out because of its unusual location, dividing the space in two. The extractor over the work table is part of a single piece with multiple functions: storage drawers for utensils, halogen lights to strengthen illumination, and an extractor for the range itself. Such placement is made for comfort, especially important if one takes into account that it is possible to read a book from the small library located just in front, seated on one of the kitchen stools.

One side of the compact kitchen area is open to the central nucleus. This layout encourages communication between both spaces. The result is a grouping of elements distributed separately but near each other to save space and gain comfort.

The structure extending above the table has its own electric generator and conceals several additional cupboards for storing food and utensils.

The compact area for cooking and for the refrigerator is located behind the central table. Some books are kept in the front part of the table, where they can be read while cooking.

Practic Loft

Berta Lozano
architect
José Luis Hausmann
photographer

This kitchen is in a 301-square-foot loft. The immediately adjacent space is a dining room/living room. An aluminum sliding door separates this space from the bedroom, the dressing room, and the bathroom. The kitchen design is notable not only for its functionalism, however, but also for its treatment. The design starts from the idea of mixing warm materials with cool ones, stained teak with aluminum. In a space by no means large, the functional mainstay of the loft accommodates in its cabinetry a washer, a dryer, a refrigerator, a microwave, a steam oven, and the ironing board.

Detail of the central table with a surface designed to be used for eating, taking advantage of the limited space in the kitchen.

Part of this kitchen's secret is that its design offers many unexpected spaces for storing all the necessities. The ironing board, the refrigerator, a ste oven, and the microwave are concealed inside.

Compact Architecture

Historically, the kitchen has been one of the most neglected rooms in the house, relegated to secondary status and always characterized by its functionality, its role in the storing, preparation, and process of elaborating food. Over time, however, sociocultural synergies have converted the kitchen into a small and unusual center for gatherings, where spaces such as the living room and the dining room are merged and where the structural parameters are blurred or even disappear to encourage communication.

This phenomena has led in recent years to a reevaluation of the kitchen and to the discovery of its rare and long forgotten beauty, as well as the many practical solutions that this space has to offer. In the kitchen, architects have found a setting that allows them to test the architectural viability of materials, textures, and designs. The kitchen has therefore become one of the most interesting fields for architects, since a variety of techniques and applications converge in this single nucleus: functionalism, design, distribution, choice of materials, technology, and even going as far as creative experimentation and provocation.

Paralleling the new leading role of the kitchen is a reduction in the traditional functions assigned to the dining room, which is becoming limited to being a space for eating. Therefore, architects consider it important to eliminate the boundaries between both areas or to combine them. One of the effects of this trend is the evolution toward a compact kitchen that includes among its virtues a nook for eating breakfast and other casual meals.

As a result of these new influences, today's compact kitchens are distilled to minimal spaces with functional amenities that fulfill all the necessities. Their materials, color, and design are a reflection of both society's eclectic nature and its evolution toward maximum practicality. With the collaboration of designers and the renewed interest of architects, the kitchen of the new millennium is becoming a magnificent space where innovative approaches demonstrate once again that the limitations of space do not present an insurmountable obstacle for architecture, much less for experimentation.

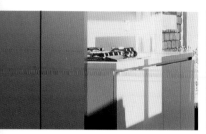

Luck Kitchen

David Luck
architect
Shania Shegedyn
photographer

Open to the exterior, the right angles of this kitchen achieve a unique volumetric result. The light is arranged to provide different intensities inside, making chiaroscuro a key element in the establishment of the ambience. The kitchen rises up in several square feet, its elements distributed in an orderly coherence. The predominant material is stainless steel, contrasting with pieces that incorporate the warmth of wood. The result is a kitchen that adapts to the maximum in the reduced space, using to advantage the opportunities offered in a kitchen facing the exterior.

The red cabinet located in the back of the kitchen is one of the most essential elements of the group. Thanks to its size, it can house a large number of the appliances and tools, keeping them organized and within reach at all times. The kitchen also includes additional storage spaces, like the top cabinets and the various drawers located in the central piece.

Carefully selected materials and the well-combined colors of the elements add lightness and a spacious feeling.

Light plays an important role in this kitchen, increasing the effect of spaciousness in the interior.

House Gaudl

Dietrich/Untertrifaller Architekten
architect
Ignacio Martínez
photographer

Next to the dining room and the living room is the kitchen of this Bregenz house. Although it is a small, closed space, there are different paths by which light enters to create a bright interior. The elements inside are distributed in an almost perfect square. The centerpiece is a simple box that determines the distribution of the rest of the kitchen elements, which remain almost unobserved due to the linearity of the surfaces. In the central box, the vitroceramics and sink are hardly perceivable in their extension via stainless-steel plate.

The rest of the elements seem to leave the attention on this central piece. The cabinets, the refrigerator, and the oven are arranged around the island, blending in with the wall. The compact surfaces exhibit very little relief. Although visually deceiving, the clean lines of these surfaces conceal more space than one would imagine.

Haus Moosman-Hämmerle

Architektur Büro DI Hermann Kaufmann
architect
Ignacio Martínez
photographer

The kitchen of this house, the property of a young couple, is inside a prefabricated box in the same space as the dining room. None of the lateral pieces or the upper part of the structure touch the ceiling or walls of the space. Thanks to this strategy, a perfect interrelationship is maintained between both independent spaces. Kitchen and dining room are clearly differentiated since the former stands out because of its intense red color.

The central hallway becomes the main and sole artery of this kitchen, which houses both the working and cooking areas. The distance between the two is minimal, but enough to make working in such a reduced space possible. The only way to leave the interior is the hallway that connects directly to the dining room, the characteristics of which are completely different from the kitchen's compact design.

Above, the red kitchen is integrated in the interior as an independent unit, contrasting with the rest of the space due to its closed, compact look.

Hecker Kitchen

Hecker Phelan Pty. Ltd.
architect
Shania Shegedyn
photographer

This kitchen is structured around a single, long, central work island that bisects the space, a very practical option in rectangular kitchens that have space to spare. Bright materials like the combination of white and black with red give the room a modern, innovative character. This is reinforced by the attractive design of the extracting hood. The counter is structured like a bar and serves the dining area as well as the work area: a modern kitchen for modern times.

One of the most noticeable aspects of this kitchen may be its horizontal layout. The faucet, the ceramic glass cooktop, the oven, the dishwasher, and the eating table are all in a line that separates this eating zone from the work space. A barely perceptible cabinet located on one side is used as a small pantry for storing food.

The work surface extends to one side to create an eating area in the small space.

The outside light increases the sense of space in the interiors, where light colors and cool materials dominate.

Haus in der Piaristengasse

Juerg Meister
architect
Pez Hejduk
photographer

This kitchen is in the middle of an irregular space, and the columns of the structure as well as the slope of ceiling further complicate the distribution of its elements. A spiral staircase in the center, leading up to the highest point of the house, is the central feature of the space. The kitchen, characterized by its compact, functional design, is actually situated to one side, taking advantage of several feet of space between the stairway and the wall. The ceiling's slope makes it possible to play with the shelf system at the back, where the oven is also located. The sink and the cooking area demarcate the front of the space, conducting the eye to the stairs, which lead to a lower level.

Totally compact and functional, this kitchen is an example of a design adapted to the architectural features of the building. The reduced area of the setting caused the architects to make use of the structure's technical advantages. They were able to isolate this kitchen from obstacles caused by certain features, like the sloped ceiling, which reduces the usable space. The result is a functional and very well thought out design.

The cupboards conform to the irregularity of the frontal structure to take advantage of every small and difficult-to-reach space.

The kitchen is located in one of the corners in the small space between the stairs and the front wall.

Tea Garden House

Stephen Varady Architecture
architect
Stephen Varady
photographer

This structure's volumes have undergone intentional manipulation to arrange the main spaces of living room, dining room, and kitchen as the highest spaces. The rooms thus flow into each other naturally.

But while the rooms communicate extremely well, they also maintain their own autonomy. The area where the kitchen is located was in fact taken from the dining area. A front window then generates flow with the remainder of the space. The result has dining room, office, and kitchen sharing a single, compartmentalized space, where each different function is strikingly partitioned off.

The shelves and the cabinets are divided between the kitchen and the front module, which serves as the eating area. The result is a compact setting that permits cooking comfortably, since everything is within reach, thanks to the clever distribution of space.

Behind the counter connected to the eating area is a hallway that leads to the kitchen, which is discreetly located in the rear.

Guests Biscuit Factory

Tom McCallum & Shania Shegedyn
architect
Shania Shegedyn
photographer

The eclectic use of materials counters the austerity of design in this kitchen. Matte colors are intercalated with polished gray metal surfaces. The resulting industrial effect is reinforced by the attractive design of the extractor, a touch of fantasy, while the three dark elements establish balance in the otherwise white module. Purity and modernity, austerity and vanguardism characterize this project, based on geometric lines and playful contrasts.

The linear appearance of the kitchen is repeated in the lateral walls. A series of barely perceptible cabinets and drawers surrounding the kitchen seem to blend into the white walls. Once again, the compact feeling results from an architectural solution that makes use of the surrounding structure.

The compact, horizontal kitchen is at one end. Meanwhile the space on the sides has been used to incorporate several extended drawers and cupboards, as seen in the above photograph.

The industrial design of the hood emphasizes the horizontal configuration of this kitchen, which barely occupies any space, since it is perfectly integrated into the surface of the wall.

  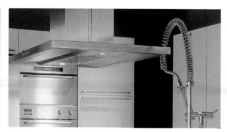 

Casa Alella

Alfons Soldevila
architect
Jordi Miralles
photographer

The central piece of furniture commands the elements in this space. A stainless-steel unit is located in the center and is the epicenter around which the rest of the kitchen furniture is distributed. The main module is thus the multifunctional element of the whole. On the one hand, it has a sophisticated plumbing system that has been specially designed for this space. The module is laterally prolonged to form a small bar counter with two stools. The design also includes a ceramic glass cooktop and a worktable with drawers, as well as the necessary cabinets for utensils.

Surrounding this central area are other elements that form part of the second tier of the setting, including vertical cabinets that encircle the module. In one of them we find the refrigerator, the microwave, the oven, and other appliances that share the same compact space.

The central module of this kitchen has enough space for neatly storing the utensils and appliances required for cooking.

Several cupboards are distributed around the central space, integrated in the setting and secondary to the dominant character of the main module.

Catalan House

Jordi Galí
architect
Jordi Miralles
photographer

Functionalism and elegance blend well in this linearly structured kitchen. The cabinets, integrated in a single module aligned along the wall, incorporate different sized drawers and multiple sub-divisions designed for storage. This makes it easy to make the most efficient use of the room's long dimensions. The polished counters of the work island are ordered, light, and functional due to the increased storage space.

Following the irregular perimeter of the kitchen, a table and four chairs for eating meals take up part of the center space. The narrow passage leading to the back of the kitchen seems to catch a breath of relief at this point, where the area opens up to increase the feeling of space.

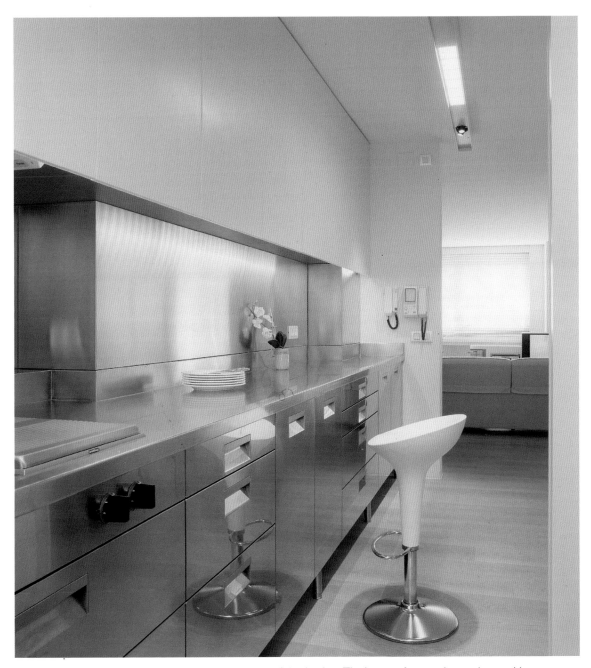

An example of the different drawers and subdivisions of this kitchen. The long surface can be used as a table at mealtime.

The Glass House

Dive Architects
architect
Jefferson Smith
photographer

Two artists bought a shell to work in and serve as their home and as a gallery space where they could exhibit their own and other artists' work. The space is defined by what has become known as a kind of "social divide": the work-sleep side versus the fun-food-relax area.

The kitchen is situated in the center of this social divide as a highly compact space. The front wall, however, is an oversized window, which floods the space with light and increases the sensation of nothing but space.

One of the main characteristics of this kitchen is its open distribution occupying a very small space. This idea results in a transparent space with a minimum number of obstacles, where only the elements of the kitchen can be seen. This space is divided into two main areas, one for cooking, with the sink, the dishwasher, and the main cabinet unit; and the worktable, which is located in the front and closes off this compact unit. The metal rack, which is an extension of the hood, hangs from the ceiling and completes this arrangement. This system keeps most of the everyday utensils at hand near the work area, making this one of the most functional and frequently used elements in this compact kitchen.

Private House Islington

Niall McLaughlin
architect
Nicholas Kane
photographer

The rustic and the industrial come together in this Niall McLaughlin project, which contrasts shiny aluminum with rough, matte white brick. A unique module of pure lines and geometrical forms drops into diaphanous space, totally free of ornamentation. The simplicity of this kitchen is stressed to the point of elegance. The lighting, carefully placed, mixes gray and white tones with blue, bringing out the absence of material.

The self-contained module for food preparation is the central feature of this space. The compact unit's clean lines and subtle materials create an object that is quite removed from the classic concept. The fixtures and the cooking elements are located in the same unit, as are the necessary cabinets for storing utensils.

The light-structured kitchen is the only central and compact system in the setting. The other elements, two benches and a table, break up the emptiness of an interior characterized by its austerity.

Revelstoke Road

Fletcher Roger Associates
architect
Paul Ratigan
photographer

This kitchen is installed under the glass structure that was added to the house to provide more space in the interior. Thanks to the small glass pavilion, the plan is able to capitalize on the light falling directly from the transparent ceiling. Cabinets and drawers are laid out in a U-shaped arrangement around a compact system of burners and an oven, designed in stainless steel. In a small space provided with a lot of light, the kitchen appears to gain in both height and amplitude, opening itself to the other rooms of the residence.

Although the kitchen functions as an enclosed unit thanks to its distribution, it was designed to encourage communication between spaces. Following this concept, a column defines the limits of one of the work surfaces, separating the kitchen from the eating area.

The cooking area presides over the U-shaped kitchen. Above, the glassed-in structure added during the remodeling takes center stage.

Mobile Compact

Compact kitchens integrated into mobile spaces, far from being an uncomfortable or impractical option, can be examples of the best functional design. By now, most land, sea, and air transportation systems have experimented with approaches to equipping their interiors with kitchens, it has been proven that living in a mobile dwelling can be a novel option, as suitable for enjoying life's pleasures as a traditional house.

The trend towards a nomadic society has captured the attention of the most progressive design sectors, which already foresee portable and collapsible structures as a response to the new demands. Despite a varying degree of opinions, flexible architecture is a central theme of progressive art, architecture, and urban design circles, which find a creative challenge for their work in the concept of mobility and flexibility.

As proof of this fact, Mobile Compact offers a selection of the most varied compact kitchens designed for modes of transportation. Each one of them is the result of a search for new, dynamic structures that are perfectly adapted to a transient lifestyle. In most cases, they fit into small spaces that encourage the design of ingenious kitchens that depart from standard models. Some of them include independent, portable elements that can be combined to configure the kitchen in stages. Others focus on an organized distribution of elements to generate an intimate space that ensures comfort in the work area. They are ideal solutions that adapt to the requirements of transportable dwellings.

In cars, in boats, in trains, and in airplanes, the kitchens prove that mobility does not impair the quality of the design, on the contrary, it becomes essential for those who travel in their architecture. If people who make alternative use of conventional spaces can be considered nomads, designing for those who transport a small kitchen will encourage creativity in this sector, and promote the use of new techniques and applications in such important spaces. The mobile compacts that follow reflect the tendency of a volatile society that in its mobility never quite becomes an integrated part of the urban fabric.

Ship·ping

Sven Everaert
photographer

The elevated structure of this boat enabled the creation of a spacious interior that distributes the different ambiences well. The owners were intent on prioritizing the living room area, which has a side that opens into the kitchen and the central table in the dining room. The kitchen's central counter includes a work island, range, and a front-opening cabinet with two portholes to filter light into the space. In the ceiling, a system of movable doors brings in fresh air.

The kitchen is divided into two parts by a central hallway, which makes it more efficient. At the back, a mirror reflects the overall layout of the ship's interior, causing it to appear larger.

Henjo

Sven Everaert
photographer

This ship, called Henjo, reflects the lifestyle of its owners. The interior is upbeat, dynamic, and changeful because they wanted no obstacles in the wide space. The walls, curvilinear in form, are of papier-mâché, and the lamps were designed by Marc Van Holden.

The compact kitchen, in a rustic style, has a stainless-steel screen that falls just above the oven, delimiting this zone from the rest of the vessel. Italian tiles accentuate the artisanal character of the kitchen, perfectly matching the overall whole, which is in the same style.

A system was designed on the surface of the hood for keeping the pots and pans in order. This not only saves space, but makes work easier, since it eliminates the need to bring them from elsewhere in the kitchen.

The rustic and artistic look of the setting is also present in this small kitchen, which barely reflects the passage of time.

Rio Claro

Sven Everaert
photographer

The Rio Claro, built in 1889, is actually a 3,767-square-foot loft that is home to a family of six. Reconstruction of the original space meant the generation and revitalization of a central space to capture the maximum amount of natural light. The system separates the day areas of kitchen, dining room, living room, and playroom from the rest of the spaces, including the bath.

The kitchen has kept the original style, with furniture recycled from the old, refurbished factories. Next to the rustic cabinets, there are several shelves for keeping objects organized. All of these elements kept in the background, clustered around the structure of the boat, emphasize the emptiness of the central space.

The small amount of space devoted to the kitchen is put to good use by a table with room for six people. Several cabinets and shelves around the perimeter, also made of wood, help keep the utensils organized.

Tia Loca

Sven Everaert
photographer

The result of the refurbishment of this boat, baptized Tia Loca, is a combination of colors that blend together in an extremely well-illuminated space. Much of the success of the blend is due to the windows looking onto the exterior. The kitchen, situated in this mobile space in a small attic, is separate from the rest of the space. The kitchen's L-shaped work island also creates an office with two stools. Thus, the cooking area is isolated but without losing contact with the other important work center.

A circular table occupies the central area. From this point, the tableware, stored on a shelf system on the front of the module, is in sight and ready for use at a moment's notice. Order and rationality are the concepts that guided the design of this kitchen, where the lack of space did not limit its possibilities.

Ankh

Sven Everaert
photographer

It took eight years to turn Ankh into a model of modernity. The great ceiling height made it possible to position the kitchen upstairs and access it via a staircase originating in the dining room. The kitchen itself is noteworthy because of its plainness; the natural tone of the wood blends with the added black. The work zone occupies only several square feet, unlike the office area, where the main elements are the centrally placed table and chairs. The work island incorporates the range and includes a complementary counter.

Various cabinets and an oven were placed on one side, using the wall that defines the kitchen. The design of a compact space incorporating all the proper functions of a kitchen was achieved through the clever distribution of its interior. The different areas were laid out keeping in mind the function and the use of each one.

Part of the central module has been converted into a complementary counter with four stools placed at it. The rest of this module, which forms a U shape, contains all the required elements: a ceramic glass cooktop, an oven, a refrigerator, and a space for storing foods.

Eco-Tech

Cuypers & Q Architects
architect
Sven Everaert
photographer

The inside of this ship reflects innovation and character, above all in the handling of the materials, especially in the built-in kitchen. Sliding doors mark this space off from the rest of the ship. The extractor hood is beautifully and subtly designed to fit into the whole, resulting in a very compressed unit whose design is cold, discreet, and extremely functional.

The goal in this ergonomic space was the integration of technological innovations within the compact kitchen, averting the need to move around a lot, as is the case of kitchens that occupy larger spaces. The cabinets in the lower part of the module blend in with the rest of the setting, concealing the fact that there is adequate space behind them to store the kitchen utensils. This practical solution takes the durability and life of the materials into account.

A movable partition was designed to help conceal the kitchen when it is not being used. This solution is made possible by the compact and built-in design of the ship's structure.

Hail Britannia!

Laurent Teisseire
photographer

This English boat, built in 1917, was rehabilitated in 1983 and at present belongs to an architect couple. The interior is distributed after the fashion of a loft, with spaces blending together to coexist in the same main room. The kitchen is at one end, in the same rustic and easygoing style as the rest of the boat. The furniture has been designed to keep all the necessary equipment in order in a space by no means large. Note the rush baskets in the shelves, a functional response that further underlines the rustic character in this area. The illumination by way of portholes was chosen to be in line with the decor.

To maximize the space, low furniture was chosen for this area of the kitchen. This way, the light coming in through the round windows creates a brighter space, free of obstacles that would break up the area. The consideration of different possibilities offered by this interior and the proper combination of materials make this a comfortable and functional space.

The various shelves and cabinets in the lower part contain baskets for storing objects in an orderly manner.

Mercator

Sven Everaert
photographer

The Mercator made its maiden voyage in the north of Europe in 1939. Below the ship's deck of African wood, the collapsible stove is perhaps the most notable industrialized element in the space. Its design makes it possible to isolate it from the other elements when it is not in use by covering it with a screen. It is a compact, stainless-steel device with an extractor hood of abstract design. Ethnic art objects around this element stand out, notably the table, chairs, and African drums.

The kitchen's interior houses many unusual spaces. At the top, a shelf runs the length of the unit, providing space to store small products and containers. The lower area is reserved for larger pot and pans, which are organized in huge drawers.

This unit is completely self-sufficient. The lower part houses small cabinets, which provide additional storage. The unit can be closed off when not in use.

The Vagaries of a River

Sven Everaert
photographer

The kitchen on this boat was designed to be installed beneath a skylight, allowing natural light to fall on the center of the area. The white presentation stands out in a space of only a few feet concentrated on one side of the boat. The two work surfaces were placed parallel to each other with a minimum distance between them to create a passageway and facilitate work activities. A wooden frame separates the rest of the boat from the kitchen zone, which distributes the light to the rest of the interior.

The oven, the dishwasher, and the refrigerator are incorporated into the wall that delimits one of the work surfaces. The unit's simple and functional lines create a kitchen that fits into a very small space but maintains communication with the other areas of the boat, thanks to the open layout of its components.

The kitchen makes good use of the different points of contact with the outdoors, like the skylight and the genuine oculus windows. This solution increases the feeling of space and provides a good source of ventilation.

Grâce de Dieu

Sven Everaert
photographer

The space of Grâce de Dieu is organized on two levels. The kitchen is in the boat's entrance, and the dining area is on an upper deck. The kitchen is notable for its contrast of cold materials like aluminum with artistic treatments and warm materials, such as the green paint used on the wall and the wood elements. Details like the relief work in the cabinets stand out, and remind us of the classic portholes of the nautical tradition. The addition of the main table enables the bar counter to link the kitchen and the dining room, a system that makes moving plates from place to place easier.

Details around the worktable demonstrate the emphasis on function and efficiency. For example, knives and other flatware are located in sight on the metal bars in front of the space. This is a kitchen that incorporates practical solutions for food handling and preparation in a mobile, compact space.

Hermit's Cabin

Arvesund
architect
Arvesund
photographer

The Swedish designer Mats Theselius collaborated with Arvesund Trädesign to design Hermit's Cabin—a cabin just big enough for one person. Hermit's Cabin is equipped for all seasons and can be located practically anywhere. In the mountains, in the woods, in your own backyard, or maybe even inside your own house: anywhere you want to create a room for a retreat and stillness.

The cabin is 81 square feet and covered inside and out with wood from old northern Swedish barns. Hermit's Cabin recycles not only materials but also history and emotions. This cabin is a way of compensating for the city dweller's lack of seclusion and proximity to nature. Here you can light a fire, eat, sleep, read, doze or, quite simply, do nothing.

The best example of a compact kitchen is the one found in Hermit's Cabin. The project has only a simple cooking area and a system for supplying water, which comes from the tank located above, which stores the required water. It is an atypical kitchen that fulfills the needs of the moment wherever the location, thanks to its mobility.

This 160-square-foot house makes a portable and cozy refuge where a small corner has been reserved for food preparation.

Directory

Alfons Soldevila, Arquitecte
Avenida Castanyer, 11
Urbanización Mas-Ram
08916 Badalona, Barcelona
Spain
Phone: +34 93 395 2854
Fax: +34 93 395 2854
www.arquitectes.coac.net/lacasatranslucida
soldevila@coac.net

Architektur Büro DI Hermann Kaufmann ZT GH
Sportplatzweg, 5
6858 Schwarzach
Austria
Phone: +43 5572 58174
Fax: +43 5572 58013
www.kaufmann.archbuero.com
office@archbuero.at

Arvesund
Arvesund Trädesign AB
Arvesund 126
830 02 Mattmar
Sweden
Phone : +46 640 440 21
Fax: +46 640 441 59
www.arvesund.com
info@arvesund.com

Cuypers & Q Architects
Bogaardestraat 10-12
2000 Amberes
Belgium
Phone : +32 3 232 48 49
Fax: +32 3 232 57 56
www.cuypers-q.be
info@cuypers-q.be

David Luck
17 Hardy Street
South Yarra
3141 Victoria
Australia
Phone : +61 3 9867 7509
Fax: +61 3 9867 7509
www.users.bigpond.com/david.luck
david.luck@bigpond.com.au

Designkoop
Johannes Kiessler
Via San Gregorio, 27
20124 Milan
Italy
Phone : +39 02 2024 1271
Fax: +39 02 2024 8014
jk@designkoop.com

Andreas Hopf
Pankgrafenstrasse, 7
13187 Berlin
Germany
Phone: +49 30 4809 5864
Fax: +49 30 4809 5865
ah@designkoop.com

Claus-Christian Eckardt
Sallstrasse, 41
30171 Hannover
Germany
Phone: +49 511 279 0881
Fax: +49 511 279 0882
www.designkoop.com
ce@designkoop.com

Dietrich/Untertrifaller Architekten
Arlbergstrasse, 117
6900 Bregenz
Austria
Phone: +43 5574 78 888-0
Fax: +43 5574 78 888-20
www.dietrich.untertrifaller.com
arch@dietrich.untertrifaller.com

Disaster Design, Alberto Colonello
Via A. Oroboni 5/a
20161 Milan
Italy
Phone: +39 02 646 4880
Fax: +39 02 646 4880
www.disasterdesign.it

Disseny d'Interiors Berta Lozano
Pau Claris 179, entlo 2.ª
08037 Barcelona
Spain
Phone: +34 93 215 58 93
Fax: +34 93 215 10 81
www.berta-lozano.com
berta@berta-lozano.com

Dive Architects Ltd.
A009 The Jam Factory
19 Rothsay Street
SE14UF London
United Kingdom
Phone: +44 20 7407 0955
Fax: +44 20 7407 7077
www.divearchitects.com
mail@divearchitects.com

Estudi Jordi Galí
Passatge Forasté 4, entlo. D
08022 Barcelona
Spain
Phone: +34 93 211 54 42
Fax: +34 93 212 26 73
jordigali@grapesadsl.com

Fletcher Roger Associates
123 Cleveland Street
W1T 6QA London
United Kingdom
Phone: +44 20 7637 1244
Fax: +44 20 7631 1191
www.fletcherroger.com
info@fletcherroger.com

Hecker Phelan Pty. Ltd.
Unit 3c/68
Oxford Street
Collingwood
3066 Victoria
Australia
Phone: +61 3 9419 0466
Fax: +61 3 9417 0866
hp@heckerphelan.com.au

Heinz A. Hellermann
Rheinstrasse 45/A6
12161 Berlin
Germany
Phone: +49 30 859 879-0
Fax: +49 30 859 879-30
www.hellermann.de
info@hellermann.de

Holger Kleine Architekten
Lützowstrasse 102-104 / Aufgang C
10785 Berlin
Germany
Phone: +49 30 253 589 30
Fax: +49 30 253 589 40
www.holgerkleinearchitekten.de
info@holgerkleinearchitekten.de

Jam Design & Communications Ltd.
4th Floor 35-39 Old Street
EC1V 9HX Londron
United Kingdom
Phone: +44 20 7253 8998
Fax: +44 20 7253 9966
www.jamdesign.co.uk
postmaster@jamdesign.co.uk

Juerg Meister
c/o nextroom - architektur im netz
Lindengasse 56/2/20
1070 Vienna
Austria
Phone: +43 1 523 32 12 - 13
Fax: +43 1 523 32 12 - 22
www.nextroom.at
office@nextroom.at

Kurt Lichtblau/Konrad Spindler
Architekten
Porzellangasse, 13/15
1090 Vienna
Austria
Phone: +43 1 319 67 46
Fax: +43 1 319 67 46-19
www.lichtblauspindler.at
office@lichtblauspindler.at

Lewis.Tsurumaki.Lewis Architects, PLLC.
147 Essex Street,
New York, NY 10002
United States
Phone: +1 212 505 5955
Fax: +1 212 505 1648
www.ltlwork.net
office@ltlwork.net

Michele Bonino
Via Sacchi, 26
10128 Turin
Italy
Phone: +39 011 5174862
studio@michelebonino.191.it

Moneo Brock Studio
Francisco de Asís Méndez Casariego 7, bajos
28002 Madrid
Spain
Phone: +34 91 563 8056
Fax: +34 91 563 8573
www.moneobrock.com
contact@moneobrock.com

371 Broadway, 2nd Fl.
New York, NY 10013
United States
Phone: +1 212 625 0308
Fax: +1 212 625 0309
www.moneobrock.com
contact@moneobrock.com

Niall McLaughlin Architects
39-51 Highgate Road
NW5 1RS London
United Kingdom
Phone: +44 0 20 7845 9170
Fax: +44 0 20 7845 9171
www.niallmclaughlin.com
info.@nialmclaughlin.com

Norisada Maeda Atelier
Glass House 1F, 1-9-5 Izumi-Honcho
201-0003 Komae-shi, Tokyo
Japan
Phone: +81 3 3480 0064
Fax: +81 3 5438 8363
www5a.biglobe.ne.jp/~norisada
norisada@sepia.ocn.ne.jp

Peanutz Architekten
Elke Knöß & Wolfgang Grillitsch
Schlesische Straße, 12
10997 Berlin
Germany
Phone: +49 030 4437 9033
Fax: +49 030 4437 9010
www.peanutz-architekten.de
post@peanutz-architekten.de

Stephen Varady Architecture
P.O. Box 105 St. Peters NSW
2044 Sydney
Australia
Phone: +61 2 9516 4044
Fax: +61 2 9516 4541
svarady@bigpond.com

Tom McCallum & Shania Shegedyn
PO Box 772
3141 South Yarra, Victoria
Australia
Phone: +61 3 4110 29 939
Fax: +61 3 9600 9168
shaniatom@optusnet.com.au